$150 REWARD

RANAWAY from the subscriber, on the night of the 2d instant, a negro man, who calls himself *Henry May*, about 22 years old, 5 feet 6 or 8 inches high, ordinary color, rather chunky built, bushy head, and has it divided mostly on one side, and keeps it very nicely combed; has been raised in the house, and is a first rate dining-room servant, and was in a tavern in Louisville for 18 months. I expect he is now in Louisville trying to make his escape to a free state, (in all probability to Cincinnati, Ohio.) Perhaps he may try to get employment on a steamboat. He is a good cook, and is handy in any capacity as a house servant. Had on when he left, a dark cassinett coatee, and dark striped cassinett pantaloons, new---he had other clothing. I will give $50 reward if taken in Louisvill; **100** dollars if taken one hundred miles from Louisville in this State, and **150** dollars if taken out of this State, and delivered to me, or secured in any jail so that I can get him again.
WILLIAM BURKE.

Bardstown, Ky., **September 3d, 1838.**

A Slave's Adventures Toward Freedom. Not Fiction, but the True Story of a Struggle

By

Peter Bruner

Prepared for publication

By

HISTORIC PULISHING

A Slave's Adventures Toward Freedom Not Fiction, but the True Story of a Struggle

By

PETER BRUNER

OXFORD, OHIO
[1918]

CITIZENS
OF
BOSTON!

A Free Citizen of Massachusetts---Free by MASSACHU-SETTS LAWS until his Liberty is declared to be forfeited by a

MASSACHUSETTS JURY, IS

Now Imprisoned

IN A MASSACHUSETTS

TEMPLE ⁞ JUSTICE!

The Compromises, trampled upon by the SLAVE POWER when in the path of Slavery, are to be crammed down the throat of the North.

THE KIDNAPPERS ARE HERE

Men of Boston! Sons of Otis, and Hancock, and the "Brace of Adamses!"

See to it that Massachusetts Laws are not outraged with your consent! See to it that no Free Citizen of Massachusetts is dragged into Slavery,

Without Trial by Jury!   '76.

I DEDICATE THIS BOOK
TO
MY CHILDREN AND GRANDCHILDREN

Introductory

In this book, I have given the actual experiences of my own life. I thought in putting it in this form it might be of some inspiration to struggling men and women.

In this great, free land of ours, every person, no matter how humble or how great seems the handicap, by industry and saving, can reach a position of independence and be of service to mankind.

PETER BRUNER.

A speaking likeness of Peter Bruner as he appeared to the students of Miami University where he served as janitor for many changing and interesting years.

CONTENTS

A Slave's Adventures Toward Freedom

CHAPTER I

I was born in Clark County, Winchester, Kentucky, in the year of 1845. I do not know exactly the month or day. My mother had two other children besides myself. Of those two one is living and the other is dead. My master's name was John Bell Bruner. I used to quite frequently see him and my mother fighting over her children. About this time I was about 8 years old.

My master was a tanner in partnership with his brother Joe. The slave traders would buy the slaves at market and take them down the river on a boat. Then he would tell them to start up a song, and then I would hear them begin to sing:

"O come and let us go where pleasure never dies,
Jesus my all to Heaven is gone,
He who I fix my hopes upon.
His track I see and I'll pursue
The narrow road till him I view.
Oh come and let us go,
Oh come and let us go where pleasure never dies."

Some of them seemed very much distressed because they had to leave their children and mothers and friends behind. Those that refused to sing they would throw that big whip in among them and make them sing. Then they would take them to Lexington where they owned a trading yard and put them in there and feed them well before the slave trader came from Now Orleans to buy them, just the same as horse purchasers came from Richmond and Cincinnati to purchase horses at Oxford. After they remained in the trading yard for 3 or 4 weeks they would ship them to New Orleans. Some few of the white people were good to their slaves and desired them to have whatever they had to eat, and would never sell them to a slave buyer. If they had more slaves than they could find employment for they would hire them out by the year to some good man who would deal justly with them.

In some cases we had there what you call patrolmen; they called them padarollers there. If they caught you off of your master's premises after nine clock at night without a pass they would whip you, and if you attempted to fight them back they would take you to the whipping post and give you 39 lashes, or sell you down the river.

CHAPTER II

When I was about 10 years old a man from Lexington by the name of Allen offered $800 for me. My master told him he would not sell me and he also stated that I was just growing into money, that I would soon be worth $1,000.

One day my master sent me from the shop to the house to procure some paste, and I forgot to bring it for him, so he whipped me with a stirrup-strap and sent me back after it. And that made me so mad, for revenge I went immediately and poured it all down my breast, which almost killed me; they had to send for two doctors to spare my life. That was the only time that he ever whipped me while I resided in Winchester.

About this time he removed from Winchester to Irvin where his brother Joe resided, about 35 miles from Winchester, so they took my sister and myself with them. After he had got us there he said he was going to break us in so then trouble began with us. When I lived in Winchester I did get good food to eat but when we moved to Irvin we did not have anything to eat but corn-bread, fat meat and water to drink, blackeye peas and greens which I gathered, and we had to eat that out of the skillets. We did not have any tables to eat upon like we do now. There were also a lot of other slaves that belonged to Joe and John Bruner in partnership. And when they did not have enough food to satisfy their hunger they would step up and take ours from us so we had to do without. The white people had plenty of the best of food but we never got any unless we stole it. Whenever they would have biscuits they would count them so they could tell if we stole any. They took me then as a house boy to nurse the children. Then I had to sleep on the floor and have nothing but a few ragged quilts to lie on and cover with also.

Just across the road from our house there lived a man by the name of Mr. Joe Clark who treated his slaves respectfully and gave them good food and good clothing to wear. Mr. Curtis was also very good to his slaves. About this time my master commenced to drink whiskey and of course he grew meaner and meaner every day. Sometimes he would come home drunk and whip all of the slaves about the place. He would hit them with anything that he got hold of.

One Saturday evening I went down to the beef club to get the beef. There were a couple of white lads at our house and one of them threw a rock and struck me with it. I put my horse up down to the tanyard and he and I went to fighting. So I whipped the boy, knocked him into a tan vat. It was at those times against the law for a colored boy to fight a white boy. The boy's father came up and told my master that he would have to whip me or he would have to take me to the whipping post and give me 39 lashes. If a white boy jumped on a colored boy and whipped him it did not make any difference how poor he was you were not allowed to touch him and besides the whipping the boy would give you your master would give you another one. There was a colored boy of Mr. Dewitt's who stabbed a poor white boy on election day. The cause of this fracas was the colored boy had gone in swimming and the white boy hid his clothes while he was in there. There were two or three hundred after him with clubs and boulders trying their very best to take his life. They ran him in a cornfield and went home. He had a very good master who went his bail which was $1,000. He kept putting the trial off until the war broke out and then he went to war. And the white boy got well again.

They took me out of the house now and put me to hard work. They made my sister and myself carry all the water and wash all the clothes every week. We had to carry the water about 350 yards on our heads in pails and you know what nice work that is. If we did not get the clothes clean my mistress would send me over to the tanyard and have my master whip me. And I let you know she examined every piece thoroughly. He had to go to town every morning to get full of that horrid, poisonous, intoxicating liquor before he was prepared to whip any person. On one wash day my mistress had him to whip me. The first thing he did was to take a piece of sole leather about 1 foot in length and 2 inches in width and cut it full of holes. Then the next thing he did was to make me undress and he had a bucket of salt water setting beside him. This was to dip that strap into, and when he was through whipping me my back was full of knots all over where those holes had been. I know my reader will sympathize with me. At nights he would have me to beat hominy. This hominy was beat out of corn. It was beat in a mortar a large piece of timber similar to a water bucket. They had a pestle to beat the hominy with. By the time I would get this beaten it would be about 10:30

o'clock and the next duty I was to perform was to go and wake my mistress up in order for her to see if it was fine enough. Then I would return and next time beat it into meal. Then I would have to go and get another peck of corn and beat it, and by the time I had accomplished this it would be about 1 o'clock I think that was good bedtime)[(] and had such a nice bed to sleep upon, old rags on the floor). When morning came my master would go to town and get drunk. Then the first thing he would do on his return was to call me up and whip me for no other purpose than because I got the hominy too fine to suit him.

One night while we were beating hominy my sister and myself thought we would change the programme, so we undertook to make a pound cake. The first thing we did was to steal out some flour and sugar. I do not know whether you call it stealing or not but it was our own labor. Then my master's brother Joe came in on us, and asked us what was in the skillet and we told him it was corn-bread. And the next thing he said was "get me a plate, I will take a piece of that." We then told him it was not done yet and he said "he would wait until it got done." We did not know what to do then, we knew it was not any corn-bread and we knew we had told a story about it also. Oh! we felt so cheap we could have taken a cent for ourselves.

He then told us to take the lid off, it was through cooking by this time and he would take a piece of it. This cake was baked in a skillet by an old-fashioned fireplace. We do not bake cakes in skillets in this enlightened age, neither do we bake them by fireplaces, but we bake them in cake pans and in ovens. He said it was a peculiar kind of cake made out of flour and sugar and that he was not used to eating that kind of corn-bread and he wanted to know whereabouts we got the sugar and we informed him that we got the flour out of the pantry and the sugar out of the sugar desk. We anticipated a whipping the next morning but he did not tell my mistress about it for he knew we did not have the pleasure of eating cake very often. But if he had informed my mistress of our cake we would have received a whipping, and a good one it would have been.

But Joe Bruner was a good natured man, he was not cruel like his brother. He never would whip me very much not more than two or three times, sometimes he would kick me every now and then, but I did not mind that for I was used to such hardships those days. They had nine or ten more colored slaves there, they were composed of men, children and one woman. They were in partnership and belonged to John and Joe Bruner both. Sometimes John and his brother would get terribly angry and nearly fight on account of the way my master treated the slaves. And he would go away from home and remain away for five or six weeks on this account. I have known them to have revolvers drawn on each other. If it were not for a man by the name of Bill Bellows interfering with them and separating them they would have ended their lives.

My master possessed one man by the name of Tandy Bruner whom he had purchased for $1,500. He purchased him from a man by the name of Mr. Johnson. Tandy was a good worker but he would not stand to be whipped. He said he would do the best he knew how, but he would not be whipped and stated that they could kill him first, and they did not whip him very often, only occasionally. He was like good old Uncle Tom. Tandy went to town one night. The patrolmen caught him down town and attempted to whip him but they did not succeed, it was just the reverse. Tandy whipped them, threw four of them into a large mud hole and then they were in a dilapidated condition when they came out. And Tandy returned home and the patrolmen never molested him any more that night.

I was down in the tanyard one day when my master came home from town and informed Tandy that he intended to whip him. He was busily engaged cleaning out a tan vat. He attempted to strike him and Tandy informed him that he would not be whipped and walked off to the house and never said another word. And my master did not trouble him and went to the house also.

One day I went to a place where they were raising a mill. There was a white man employed by the name of Jerry Cox. He took it on himself to tell Tandy that he was not lifting enough. So he threw down his hand spike and proceeded to whip him. Then Tandy gave him one of the most severe thrashings that he ever had. Tandy was a fellow that would not take any foolishness. The building in the tanyard was a very large building, it had three stories. Joe Bruner took him up there and locked the doors and pretended that he was going to whip Tandy, but he did not touch him Tandy said afterwards, and the people never knew the difference.

Tandy had for his wife a woman by the name of Dulceny Bruner and she and Tandy could not agree so they separated. They had a little girl by the name of Amandy. She was hired out to a man by the name of Mr. Price, down town. And one day as Tandy was passing by there, his wife sent her little girl Amandy to take him some cakes, so he took them and ate them, and about an hour after that he took sick about two miles from home, driving a four-horse wagon. He had gone out after a load of wood accompanied by two little boys. He died within three days and before he died he stated that there was something on him like a large bear or dog and asked his master to pray for him, and he was nothing but a big black sinner himself. Tandy died a terrible death. After he died they cut him open and found out that he had been poisoned. They intended to hang his wife and then they thought they could not prove it on her, and then they thought they could not afford to lose two slaves at once so they never did anything with her. Oh how many deeds that are committed never receive punishment. But there is a day when all deeds shall be punished.

CHAPTER III

My master owned another man by the name of black John. He was always in trouble, he was always fighting and he would steal the hat off of a man's head if you did not watch him very closely. They always trusted him with four horses and a wagon. He hauled leather to Lexington and Winchester to sell. One trip would be about 30 miles and the other about 41 miles.

Black John was a good scholar. He could read and write and that was something more than we could do. I do not know how he learned to read and write. He was a skillful hand for breaking into some man's smoke house and procuring all of their meat, and you never could catch him; and after he had obtained the meat he would always sell it to some white man. One time he took his departure from home and forgot to come back, and he has not returned to this day. Where he is no person ever knew. We did hear from him once, when he left our town he took away about $500 worth of property and money. He is now in Canada and is doing well. This was about 38 years ago. He owned a wholesale store in that place. He wrote back to his master and told him if he would come there he would pay him for all the damage he did while on his plantation. They thought once that they would go after him and bring him back home and then they thought it might not be a safe plan so they never molested him. I have never heard of his death, and I am not bothered much about him, for he will not aid me any by knowing.

Now the next thing I will proceed to relate is the way they conducted the election. They had no schools there whatever for the poor white people, their aim was to keep them ignorant as long as they possibly could. About two or three weeks before the election they would give them a little work. On our plantation there were three and four hundred cords of wood to cut and also about three or four hundred cords of tan bark to be peeled. (They only paid 25 cents a cord for cutting wood and 50 cents a day for peeling bark.)

The elections generally came on the first Monday in August. Then my master and a few more of the leading Democrats would go out and electioneer. Then they would have these low-class of people to come into the building there at the tanyard and they would play cards and drink whiskey all night. And the next day they would take them down and vote them. And my master and those other men would have no more use for them until next election day. After that I have known them to come to our house to purchase some leather for the purpose of making their children some shoes who were without them. And they did not have the money at that time to pay for it, but my master would not let them have it under any circumstances. He had procured their votes and what did he care for those men then. This is the way they carried their elections there.

At that time I was a Democrat myself, but you see I have changed now. I went in front of the column carrying a long hickory pole with a large red handkerchief attached to it. The colored people would sometimes give these poor white people a piece of meat or a peck of cornmeal when they would say that they did not have anything. We always kept very bad dogs at our house. Sometimes these poor people would come and steal the meat from the smoke house (they had no way to lock it) and would get but a little distance away with it before our dogs would be after them, and they would climb up the trees and then my old master would be aroused by this time. He would make them take it back and give them a whipping beside. So they would not gain much after all. I am afraid they were the losers.

The reason why there were so many poor white people there was on account of the iron furnace they had there. They had come there from another country. You could travel ever so far and you could see no fences and the land would not be cleared up; they had abundant forests there and all they had to do was to enter into the woods and cut down the trees and build them rude huts. And they were rude huts, too. They had no floors in their houses, simply the ground and did not have any chairs, but had long benches instead. They did not know anything about church, they never were seen going there. Instead of going to church where they might have been benefited by hearing the word of God, they would go hunting and fishing. That was their occupation on Sunday; they were more like heathens than anything else. There were three things that they were well versed in and that was drink whiskey, fight and kill people. I have seen as many as twenty and thirty fighting at once. Sometimes they would strike you over the head with a weight.

Most of their work was to cut hoop poles and dig iron ore; some of them would only work when they would have high tide on the river. They would help load up pig iron, and some of them did not do anything, and some would cut up barrel staves, and raft saw logs together. There were several still houses there and that is all these poor people wanted. They would spend the last cent they had for that ruinous, intoxicating drug which ruins so many families.

By this time they had put me in the tanyard to work, to a man's work, for the purpose of laying away leather, clean out tan vats, wheel out tan bark and handle the heavy hides in the beam-shop, taking them out of the vats called limes. And when a pack of leather was tanned I would have to carry it upstairs to be scoured out. About three days in the week I had to run the engine and tend to the mill and every evening I would have to go out in the mountains in search of the cows, the time for me to do this was about 4 o'clock. And when I would not be successful in finding them they would send me again for them way after dark, like I could see a cow in the mountains long after dark where they would roam ever so far.

Whenever any misfortunes would befall us at the mill, a belt would fly off or anything like that, my master would always convict me of the charge and would whip me so severely, it got to be nothing but whippings all the time now.

When I would take the right toll out of the corn, the sack would contain just as much then as it did before it was ground. He would have me to take five toll dishes out of three bushels of corn, where there should only have been three, that was all the law allowed. And if I did not take out five he would whip me for it, punish me for doing right. I would tell him sometimes that I wished he would kill me at once and I would be done suffering in this world. He went to town that night and when he came back he cowhided me until the blood streamed down my back. He was mad because I said I wished he would kill me, but he was full of whiskey every time he did this.

One Christmas morning he was returning from town and so I thought I would catch his Christmas gift; it was always customary in those days to catch peoples Christmas gifts and they would give you something. Instead of giving me the kind of Christmas present I desired, he took me and threw me in the tan vat and nearly drowned me. Every time I made an attempt to get out he would kick me back in again until I was almost dead. At last I came up on the other side and jumped out before he was able to get around there.

Sometimes he would tell us to go to church but that was not very often. But we were not benefited any by going, we did not hear anything but "servants obey your master." That is what was preached to the slaves. He thought that was all that was necessary for us to hear.

My master's employment on Sunday was to go fishing and he would take me with him, and he would take a large bottle of whiskey with him for company. I have known some of those slave holders to go to church on Sunday and would pretend to be so good while they were there, and no sooner than they had arrived at home they would commence to whip some of their slaves. And some of them would have their slaves hauling fodder all Sunday forenoon to feed the cattle on. So one night I went down town and did not ask him and when I came back that night he took me off of my pallet and took me out to a barrel full of water and stuck my head in it with my heels sticking up. This almost drowned me. I thought I was nearly drowned when I came out, but as it happened I was still living.

One evening they sent me down on the other side of town to take mules to the pasture; and on my way back they had the patrolmen to catch me. It was about half past eight o'clock. So these patrolmen caught me and whipped me. Their object in doing this was to keep me from going to town, they wanted to break me in. But they did not succeed for after this occurred I went to town every night.

At night the aristocrats would come in to see my master and mistress for the purpose of playing euchre and remain until one and two o'clock. One night they came there, took a notion that they wanted some apple jack. So they sent me down to Dr. Shell's drug store to get the whiskey and apples. I took a notion that I wanted a drink like the aristocrats. I asked his son Alfred to give me a drink and he asked me how much I could drink, I told him a goblet full, so he gave it to me and I drank it and it made me drunk, and on the way home I lost the jug of whiskey and my apples. And the next thing I knew the children were on me riding and whipping me just the same as if I had been a horse or some other dumb animal. So the white people did not get any apple jack that night and, I got it all.

Soon after this it came the time to gather ice. We had a very large ice house at our house. A man by the name of Nelan went in partnership with him to help fill it. About two or three weeks after they had succeeded in filling the ice house, Mr. Nelan and my master could not agree, so they fell out. They commenced fighting and he shot my master and put two or three balls into him. It did not kill him but I was terribly sorry that it did not. Then they took me into the house to wait on him and you know that was pleasant work. And when the least little thing did not go to suit him he would call me up to the bed and proceed to whip me with a large stick or maybe a cowhide. He would even strike me when his pains would hurt him. I wanted him to die but it seemed like he would not die. He is dead now at the time I write this but he did not die until all of the slaves were taken away from him.

Now I am going to tell you about a little trick I played, but I payed very dearly for it before it was finished. It was not my fault though. I came upon a fellow by the name of Henry Wagle down to the Estle springs. He had shot a cat and skinned it, so he gave it to me and told me it was a rabbit. So I met Alfred Myers and told him if he would give me a nickel and let me ride to town I would let him have the rabbit. So we traded and the boy took it home and the next morning his parent cooked it for breakfast. So they ate the cat and his daughter declared that it had the finest liver that she had ever seen, and also stated that it was a very good rabbit. I guess it must have been a young cat or they surely would not have relished it so much. They would never have known it if Henry Wagle had not told them any better. He went down town and heard them boasting about what good rabbit they had. After old Milt Myers found it out and told my master that he would have to punish me in some way. So my master told me be would have me taken clown to the whipping post and get a whipping. So that would not do he must whip me himself. They took me down there and he gave me one hundred lashes and the white fellow got away unpunished. So that ends the cat story.

The next bad deed that I did was I went down town one day and got into a fight with a fellow by the name of Fount Suel, and I shot him with a little single barrel pistol loaded with beans. It did not hurt him, it just made a little blood come. Then about 25 men commenced fighting over that. The next morning Joe Bruner had me taken down to the whipping post where I was to receive 39 lashes, but the remaining portion of the fellows were not there so I escaped uninjured.

It always fell to my lot to do all of the trading and we always run a bill lasting from one year until another. So I thought I would get even with the white people. I thought I would go down and get one dollar's worth of maple sugar. It sold at 10 cents a cake and so I received ten cakes and charged it to the white people, and enjoyed those cakes and don't you forget it I ate them in three days. I ate them up in a mountain under a pine tree, which you know was very pleasant. When Christmas arrived they looked over the account and saw the sugar recorded there but they were under the impression that they had purchased the sugar themselves and there I had enjoyed that all to myself. One day I went down on White Oak to old Miss Patsy White, where the colored people held meeting. A Baptist preacher was preaching. I was sitting on a fence post directly in front of the stand, they held their meeting in the yard. So he was preaching about Peter and pointing his finger at me, I thought he was talking about me and it made me very angry, and I cried out I did not do any such a thing and called him an old liar, and then jumped off of the post and returned back to town. By this time my old master had regained his health and had returned back to the tanyard meaner than ever.

About this time we bad a large quantity of corn to grind. We ground it for the furnace hands and of course they expected me to do the work of two hands. So he began to whip me more and more every day. He would go down town and get full of that poisonous liquor, and we all know when whisky is in, wisdom is out. We always let our horses graze out on the commons, and about a half mile from our house was the Sulphur Springs, which were owned by old Billy Childs at that time. So they sent me after the horses and I was driving them back. They did not have any bridles on, so old Mrs. Childs came out on the road on horseback going to town. The horses kicked up so very much dust they would be behind her, then they would run around in front of her, and kick up dust. And Mrs.

Childs was dressed in a very nice black silk dress, and of course she hated to have it soiled but I could not stop the horses from running, if I could have I would, for you know how much dust a drove of horses makes. Mrs. Childs was very angry indeed and in return she had me to come in and take off my coat and vest and had all of her slaves come in and look at me while she cowhided me. I do not know how many lashes she gave me but I do know that she whipped me a long time. I tried to persuade the boys to let me loose but they would not. I even offered them my old pen knife which I had stored in my pocket, but all in vain, they would not yield. My master talked of making them pay for it, but he did not once put his talks into execution.

One day it was very very dry and we had a large amount of corn to grind for a lot of people from the mountains and some of them had conveyed it ever so far on their backs. And it seemed like everything had gone wrong that week, some of the belts had flown off and my old master had gone to town and purchased some more whiskey which he drank immediately and which took effect as soon as he had partaken of it. And when he returned he then commenced whipping me. So when he went to the house to eat his breakfast, Mr. Sheppard and Rollins and some more fellows told me if they were me they would run off and go to the free state. So when night came on I took a notion that I would run off, and out I started to a free state. But I happened to go the wrong road, and the first thing I knew I was in Richmond, Kentucky, in Madison County. I arrived there about eleven o'clock in the day.

I went to the woods and wandered around there till it was nearly night. I then started out on the Lexington pike, the one leading from Richmond to Lexington. So I proceeded on my way until I found myself about two miles from Clays Ferry where I stayed all night at a widow woman's house. I told those people that I was a free man and informed them that my name was Dick Kieth; I knew a fellow that was free by that name and so I thought I would assume his name. I also told them that I was on my way to Lexington. So a man came along with a large drove of horses and mules. I made a contract with him to go down to New Orleans with him and I went on to Lexington with him and his drove of horses, and there I gave him the slip. That night I went to Phoenix Hotel and called for my supper, and at that place I also gave my name as Dick Kieth and a free man, too. The waiters gave me my supper in the kitchen. While I was enjoying my supper a white man came down and wanted to know whereabouts I came from and wanted to know my name, and I told him the same thing, that my name was Dick Kieth and was free, and he then wanted me to show him my free papers. I then told him I did not bring them with me, that I had left them at home (for I did not have any to bring). He then wanted to know if there was any person here that knew me and I told him to go up in the office which was full of men, and ask them if they did not know me and while he had gone to seek information I skipped out and left that hotel. I knew this man but he did not recognize me. He was foreman at the Estle springs not far from our house. (All this time my master was looking everywhere for me, and he even searched my mother's and grandmother's house for me in Winchester, and he had spies out in every direction. But I did not even go towards Winchester. I took another route.)

Equipped with the fastest steed of days past, Peter Bruner was the fleet and much-wanted messenger "boy" of Miami University folks.

Enjoying the Sunset Years of Life, Mr. and Mrs. Peter Bruner, as They are Today.

The Best Gift Life Has to Offer, a Happy Family.

So I went out in the town of Lexington and walked around until about one or two o'clock and then I became sleepy and went and climbed in a stage and remained there all night. Next morning I got up and went out and wandered around until I came to a railroad which I had never seen before. I saw a train approaching, and I had it in my head that all of the trains went to the free state, In the meantime there was a freight train standing on the track waiting to be unloaded. It contained horses and cattle. So I climbed up there between the two trains where they were attached together and seated myself there for a half hour, and kept waiting and waiting for the engine to hitch on and pull me out, and the train had already passed and I was getting down every now and then looking for the train, and I might have been sitting there yet. So at last I became tired and thought I would get down and look for the train which had passed long ago.

I thought I was going to the free state, and the train had gone clear out of my hearing. I then began to wander around town again, and a man came up and told me that I was a runaway slave and took me before the Magistrate and swore that I was a runaway. They then asked me what my name was and I told them as I had told them before and that I was free born also. Then they took me and put me in jail. The man that had charge of the jail was named Mr. Lulsby, and the colored follow that conveyed our food to us was named Henry. About two days after I had remained there in came two men with a leather strap and a cat-o'-nine-tail. When this hit you once you got 9 lashes. He was going to whip me and make me tell him who I belonged to and what my name was. But I did not wait until they struck me one lick I cried out that I belonged to John Bell Bruner and that my name was Peter Bruner. They then wrote a letter to my master and informed him that they had me and I remained there about two weeks.

While I was in jail I had for company two of John C. Brackenridge's slaves. What they were in there for I did not learn, but we had good times anyway. They were about my size. They had a large lot with a large brick wall around it and they would let us stay in there all day and lock us up in the cells at night. And in about two weeks Joe Bruner came after me and asked me if I wanted to go back home and I told him I would rather he would sell me down the river than go back home, but you see I did not get my choice. Joe Bruner had to pay forty dollars for me for jail fee and for the catching of me. They took me out and started me to walking and said I could go by Winchester and see my mother. So I stayed there two or three days. While I remained there she presented me a penknife.

I went from there to Frank Emerson's, my mistress' father, about nine miles from Winchester. The knife which my mother gave me got me into trouble while I remained there. He had a very nice watermelon patch so I thought I would try my new knife on them, and I plugged about a dozen or more which were all green and so I turned them over the plugged side down towards the ground. I was not looking for green melons, I was looking for ripe ones. So old man Emerson got after me with an old crooked cane which he had and he ran me and ran me, but all in vain. At last I ran in the house and he shut the door, then he had me. He beat me and beat me with that old cane until I did not feel very good.

Then Joe Bruner came along and took me up to Irvin my home. We arrived there that night. I did not see my old master that night, and the next morning I got up and went out with the rest of the boys to cut wood, in the woods. So the next evening while I was out to the stable feeding the horse of Mr. Garret, who was visiting there, John Bruner who had just arrived home from town came past the barn and saw me in there and he came in and told me to come to the house that he wished to settle with me. So when he came into the stable I started to run out and he picked up a large stone and threw at me and cut me in the head, the scar remains there yet. I ran and he told the other slaves to run after me and I ran through a gang of Irish fellows, and informed them that I was going, to the river and drown myself. I did jump in and went about two or three hundred yards and came out again. The Irish fellows came down to the river looking in it for me, they supposed that I had drowned myself. I came back again over the Sweet Lick mountain, where my sister gave me a hat and something to eat. It was about ten o'clock in the night. Dan Ridle cut my hair and put some balsam or something else on it. This fellow lives at Xenia, Ohio. When this was written, he did not go by that name.

Then I wandered around and the slaves gave me something to eat whenever they had a chance.

I then went out and stayed with the poor white people in the mountains. My master looked and looked for me but all in vain, they did not succeed, so they gave up their search. Sometimes I would be no more than two hundred yards from him and sometimes I would be sitting down at these poor white peoples house enjoying my dinner and my master would ride along the ridge, He told all the slaves, ours and other peoples, too, if they saw me to tell me if I would come home he would not whip me, that he would hire me out to a Mr. Sheppard. They told me and I came in on Sunday morning while he had gone to town for his whiskey and procured my bed clothes and I went to Mr. Sheppard. When I had got about a mile from home I had stopped to talk to a colored fellow by the name of Tom Myers. While I was talking to him I happened to look back and behold there came my master after me.

Before he got to me he asked me if I had my bedclothes with me and I told him I did have them with me and he then told me to get upon the fence and he would take me to Mr. Sheppard's. He came up and grabbed me and had another fellow to hold his horse while he tied my hands behind me and took me back home. When he had arrived at home he took me into a room and undressed me and bucked me, which is tying my hands together and running my hands over my knees and then run a stick through them and that left me entirely helpless without any use whatever of myself. Then he cowhided and cowhided me until the blood stood in pools on the floor. Well I guess he whipped me for about three hours, and his wife never told him to stop once but urged him on; the more I begged the harder he would whip me and when he was through whipping me I was so sore that I could hardly walk.

After this everything went along very smoothly until one day the cows got lost and I had to go and search for them. They had gone to Clarke County about thirty miles from where we lived. The reason they always went there was because we had purchased them of Mr. Emerson. I was gone about three or four days, so when I returned home he started to whip me for staying from home so long and I ran around the hill. In those days if he just looked at me I would commence to run, you know catching is before whipping.

By this time Christmas was approaching and I cut all of my wood for Christmas, and when Christmas arrived he promised to give me my first pair of boots. I had never owned a pair of boots before. This pair was made out of white leather, it had never been blacked. I was so very proud of them I did not know what to do, so of course I had to go some place to show them. I thought I would go up to a town by the name of Procter, about twenty-five miles up the river. So I went up there and had a jolly time indeed. I went to quilting parties and dances and drank whiskey (you see I took after my master in those days). I stayed there all Christmas. The day I started home was a cold New Years day, and when I arrived at home my old master was lying there; he had been to town and had got full of whiskey while he was there. They had me pull off my boots and stand up in the chair and tell them where I had been. He told my sister to go and look for the cowhide that he intended to whip me. My sister obeyed and went in search of it and succeeded in finding it, but after she found it she did not bring it to him but she hid it and came back and told him that she could not find it. About that time the cook came and told them that supper was ready and they all went out to supper. While they were into supper I ran out and ran down to Mr. Clark's barn and stayed there in some hay all night. I did not have any hat, coat nor boots on and there was snow on the ground. My master looked for me half of the night but did not succeed in finding me. So I escaped a whipping that night, but it would have paid me best to have taken the whipping that night for I received a harder one that next morning, one for running off and the other for going to Procter, but he said I might go and I do not see why he would want to whip me.

He then thought he would hire me out to a man up the river (by the name of Jimmy Benton, a still meaner man) to break me in. So that man came and hired me and took me home with him. I was between seventeen and eighteen years old at this time. After I was there about a week I thought I would try him. He always tried to make me ask him when I went away from the house but I did not do it, I thought while he was breaking me in I would break him in.

I had just been there one week and on Sunday night I went down to his father's house, not very far from there, and did not ask him. So the next morning he told me to go out and get some switches to whip myself with, but I told him that was something I did not do for my own master, and then he jumped on me and I got the best of the old fellow, and his wife jumped out of bed with the rifle and she ran to him with it and I got hold of it and it went off some way or other. All of this occurred about four o'clock in the morning, it was not day yet. The next thing he told me to do was to go down to the barn and feed the stock and while I was employed in doing this he and his brother ran in and grabbed me. I tell you they downed me this time. They tied me up by my hands to a horse rack, and then they both procured two long black hickory switches and one whipped me on one side and one on the other. They must have given me one hundred and fifty lashes or maybe more. When they let me loose I started for home and old Jimmy Benton was riding behind me persuading me to go back.

When I arrived home the first man I saw was old Bruner down to the tanyard. He asked me what was the matter and I told him hell was to pay this morning. He then said if I would go back and remain until Christmas he would give me ten dollars. So I returned back and remained a little while longer.

I then took a notion that I would run off again. I still wanted to be free. I only wanted to get on free soil, so I started one morning between two and three o'clock and traveled ten miles on the road that night and then I hid in the bushes. The next day I went on through Madison County near Sugar Creek. I do not know what part I was in then. This was about the year of 1861, the war had begun then.

Burnside was at Camp Nelson just preparing to start out and I thought if I could only make it to that place I would be all right. Previous to this I had overtaken some more men and they were going along with me. Just as we were putting our shoes on after we had been wading the river, some five or six men came and captured them all but me and I escaped by taking refuge under some bushes. I do not know who these men were. After they had been gone about a half hour I thought I would proceed so I went on until I had gone about a half mile, then I climbed over a fence and laid down in some tall weeds. When I awoke some men were cutting the weeds over me and some of them said kill the d----

n nigger. Then they took me up to an old blacksmith's shop where they had the remaining part of the crowd. Then they took us from there to Nickleville which was about eighteen miles below Lexington. There they took us before the Magistrate and swore that we were runaway slaves. They then took us to jail. In the room I occupied were twenty-four more slaves all running off trying their very best to get free. Oh, how hard some of us poor slaves labored to gain our freedom.

A while after we were there they wrote for my master to come after me. After a week Joe Bruner and his nephew came and told me they wanted me to go home and I told him I would not go home. He then went out and purchased a cotton rope and his intentions in buying this was to tie me behind the buggy like people do their horses. And then I came to the conclusion that I would go with him, I thought the best plan would be to go along with him.

On our way from Nickleville he took me to his sister's, Elizabeth Muer, and there I remained all night. She said she wanted to buy me for the sole purpose of whipping me; she said if she could whip me and break me in she could stop me from running off. She went and got a lock and chain and locked me to a post on the porch. She would not let me come in the house and then she was afraid I would run off, Joe Bruner told her he did not think I would run off but she thought it the safest plan to lock me to a chain so she would have me.

While I remained at that house I saw a house where she whipped her slaves. She had large staples driven in the floor, then four large rings were in them and straps to strap you up. And one day while I was residing there she sent two little children between nine and ten years old to gather beans, and they happened to remain a little longer than the appointed time, so she took these little girls and cowhided them terribly right before my eyes. And out in the back yard two little boys were churning and they did not agree on something and commenced fighting and old Tom Muer came up and kicked them and beat them around. All of this brutality occurred in one day.

The next morning I went by Winchester to see my mother on my way home, and the first man I beheld was old John Bruner. I always made a great mistake every time I ran away. I always took the wrong direction. Instead of going north to the free states I went farther and farther south, just the opposite direction from which I wanted to go. Previous to this, on his way from Lexington to Nickleville going after me, Joe Bruner met three men running off, so he captured these and took them to jail at Nickleville, but there was not enough room there for them so he took them back and put them in the jail at Lexington. And he received forty dollars for this which was enough to pay the jailer fees and the men who had pursued and captured me. One of the slaves belonged to Scott, the other I do not know to whom he belonged.

When I met my old master at Winchester he simply asked me where I had been and I informed him that I had been walking about. He did not speak to me cross, neither did he look at me in the same way for he knew if he did I would be gone again, for it was my chief delight to run off. Then he took me back to Irvin and then Jimmy Benton came and took me back to his house again, but he did not whip me this time, I guess he thought it the safest plan to let me alone. He rented a large field in the bottoms and I remained there and got along nicely farming, and in turn he gave me a nice large watermelon patch and a portion of ground on which I raised thirty bushels of corn, and then he hauled it off for me and received for it one dollar per bushel which amounted to the sum of thirty dollars. I tell you I was proud, I had never had so much money before in my life.

Jimmy Benton rented a large field from widow Broaders about a mile from home, and it was my duty to break up this field with oxen. This field contained about 100 acres. John Cockrel rented about half of this field. He had a colored fellow employed by the name of Phil Stocton, who resided in the same town that I did. So one day Phil and I made up our minds that we would run off and go to the free state.

The people in our town were taking their slaves to Old Richmond, Va. So one day be and I were plowing in a field about a mile from the house when we took a notion all at once. The white people were walking around and whispering all through the night and of course, we did not know but what they were pursuing us, but we were mistaken. We then left Red River and then went up to Black Creek, and after we had gone two or three miles up Black Creek we spied a colored fellow hoeing corn and we went to him and when we had reached him we found it was a fellow that I was well acquainted with. He formerly was owned by Mr. Grabs who resided upon Miller's Creek, very near to the place from where I had run off. Phil and myself made a bargain with this fellow that we would remain there two or three days and help him hoe that corn if he would furnish us our food.

Everything was just the way we wanted it. It was in our favor for Mr. Stewart, this man's master, had gone somewhere and would be gone for several days and this was about a half mile from the road and was surrounded by woods on every side except one. And there was not anything on this side and we had an excellent view and could see to the road and house and whenever we spied anyone coming we could conceal ourselves in the woods. Everything had gone in our favor until the white man returned home and had heard of Phil and myself running off and he was speaking of it at the house but he never dreamed that we were under the roof of his house. So this colored man told us that we had better take our departure and he prepared us some food to take along with us and about midnight he awoke us up and told us in what direction he thought the North was and so we then started for the free state.

At daybreak next morning found us nearly to Mt. Sterling, Ky. Next morning we went right through town and Phil took one side of the street and I took the other and we went straight through town whistling like we had resided there all our lives, although it was our first visit to the town and they had market going on the same time. After going through town two or three miles we came to a large rack of rails and we had arrived at a strange part of the town and thought we would camp there and so we laid down here to take our rest. When night came on we resumed our journey, we were now on the Maysville pike.

When we had nearly reached Sharpsburg we came upon some colored fellow who belonged to Williams and we persuaded him to procure us some food. So he succeeded in getting some corn-bread and an old ham bone for us, but it tasted to us as good as if it had been pound cake. And on a Sunday morning I came upon a young colored fellow and tried to persuade him to go with us but we did not succeed. So I tried to gain all of the information from him that I possibly could and learned who a great many of the people were. So we went on two or three miles until we came to a large cornfield.

This cornfield covered about a mile from Sharpsburg, and about the center of this field was a locust grove and a great many sheep occupied this grove. This was a very pleasant place indeed to lie down, and while we were lying there asleep a couple of men rode upon us. So they awakened us up and wanted to know what we were doing there, and I told them that I had driven the white folks to church in a carriage. They then wanted to know who I belonged to and I informed them that I belonged to Mr. Williams and another white man that I had learned his name from that colored fellow. They then asked me if I had seen any men go through the cornfield and I jumped up and told him about two hundred yards from here I had seen a fellow running through the field and he then asked me what kind of looking fellow he was and I told him he looked to be a heavy set fellow with a white hat on. So they started out in the direction that I had told them as fast as they possibly could, and this was a great relief to me. I had never seen any one.

Then Phil and I jumped up and went through town and passed a hotel just exactly like Mayor Davis,' now the Spinning Wheel (in Oxford, Ohio), and there were ten or twelve men sitting out there in front of the hotel and we went on kind of whistling as if we had lived there all the time. We went on and did not pay any attention to them nor they to us. And when we had gone out of town we began to get hungry and we turned to the left and came up into a large apple orchard; the limbs were hanging full of ripe apples, and I tell you they looked tempting. So we filled our pockets and our breast full and then we were ready to leave that orchard. We went on a little distance farther and came to a large rack of rails. This was a splendid place to hide ourselves.

We then started and went down on the Cynthiana pike about a mile. We stopped at a wealthy white lady's house. She was a widow by the name of Hawkins and she had some slaves. She was quite a nice woman. She gave us our supper and we told her that we belonged to Mr. Williams who lived on the other side of Sharpsburg. After leaving there we turned and went back the Maysville pike. We were then coming towards the

Ohio River. We went about two miles and then stopped in an old barn and went to sleep.

We overslept ourselves; it was an hour before day when we awakened. We jumped up and on looking around we discovered an old gray horse. Phil and I both mounted him and rode for a mile coming to a toll gate which we found locked. We had to turn the horse loose for their was no way to get through it. We saw a colored man passing and we went to the road and stopped him. We told him about our condition, that we were going to the free states. He promised to bring us something to eat after dark but never returned, and I thought and always will think that he betrayed us, although he told us how to go to a mill and cross in the mill dam and get out through the mill. We climbed through the window and came out on the other side. About 9 o'clock we ventured out and following his direction we crossed in perfect safety. I told Phil that I would go ahead and he must follow about 20 yards behind me. We got almost through the town of Sheridan, when I looked back and saw two or three men. We found afterwards that they were white for one of them grabbed Phil. Thinking I could fool them by pretending that I lived in the town I commenced to whistle and started in the gate that led to a fine residence, but they caught me.

They then took us both back to a large building and took us up in the third story to a large room that looked very much as if it was a lodge room by the things it contained. They then brought their revolvers and whiskey and tried to persuade us to drink it. Their purpose was t make us drunk so they would not have any trouble. Phil drank a little but I would not touch it. I attempted to jump out of the window as I preferred death to slavery. They caught me and tied us both and guarded us until the next morning. They then brought us our breakfast and told us they were Nigger Catchers and that was the way they made their living, they said that they could tell when a slave had run off. After we ate our breakfast they handcuffed us and took us to Flemingsburg.

There was a little town between Sheridan and Flemingsburg called Pinhook. They stopped there and gave us some water to drink. They told us we were almost to the Ohio River and if they had not caught us we would have reached the Ohio River by 1:20 o'clock the next morning. They took us before the Magistrate and swore that we were runaways. Then they asked us who our masters were and I told them the truth for the first time since we had started on our journey. They took us to the jail and the room they put us in was iron and the chairs were iron and the bed was iron. We told him that Phil belonged to Mr. Stocton and I to John Bell Bruner in Irvin. The turnkey's name was Mr. Bowman and he was very good to us. We remained in jail about two weeks and on the first Monday in August, John Cockrel came after us. The man that Phil belonged to came on Jimmy Benton's horse. He had to pay eighty dollars apiece for us or we would be sold.

The evening that he came he said that we ought to be killed and he guessed he would kill us before he got through with us. Phil began to beg and plead and said he would not have run off if it had not been for me persuading him to go with me. And I told him that I would rather he would kill me than to take me back home and that it did not make a bit of difference with me what he did with me, I would as lief die now as any other time.

The next morning when John Cockrel came in the jail after us he whipped Phil and myself both with a cowhide before he took us out of the jail. Then he took out of his saddle bag a large new chain and two locks. He then locked one end of the chain around Phil's neck and the other around my neck and then we were locked together. Then he took our shoes off and put them into his saddle bag and he said that he intended to wear all of the skin off of our feet before we reached home. Now judge for yourselves how it would be walking along that distance--barefooted.

Every few hundred yards he would whip us that cruel way until we had reached our destination. Whenever he would have to stop over night he would just lock us up in a bareroom with no bed to sleep on or chairs to sit on, and he told the people where we stopped, that he did not care whether we had anything to eat or not and all the time we were in there Phil and myself were still locked together. He never unlocked us.

Just before we arrived at Red River Phil was begging him and told him he would not have run away if it had not been for me. So Phil told him that I had a half pint of whiskey in my pocket which a colored fellow had given to me at Mt. Sterling. As soon as Phil told him that he tried to make me give it to him and I took the bottle out of my pocket and drank it up and threw the bottle away and told him he could have the bottle if he went after it. And when I refused to give him the whiskey he then rode up and gave me about fifty lashes with the cowhide which did not feel extra good. When we arrived at the river he made us wade. It was more than waist deep, I guess it came up to our arms. By this time I had become mad at Phil for telling so many tales on me and while he was under the water I attempted to drown him and beat him, but I did not succeed.

At last we reached Irvin and he took us on by home and put us in jail. The only thing I hated about it was that he took me by my girl's house in that condition. She worked for Mr. Smith and her name was Mandy Suel. So Phil and I were not on very good terms any more, so they had to put us in different cells. My master came in jail that evening and asked me what did I think ought to be done with me and I told him I did not care what he did with me. So he had a blacksmith to come in that evening and take the measure around my neck, he intended to have an iron yoke made to go around my neck, and extend out about eighteen inches, then extend up sixteen inches, and he was going to have a bell fastened to that so whenever I ran away he could hear the bell ringing, and by that way I would not be able to get very far before they would catch me.

Old Bruner did not come into the jail any more until the next morning. That night some of my old partners came in and gave me some whiskey, so in the morning I was prepared to talk. The next morning my master came in, drunk as usual. I told him if he put that yoke on me I would jump into the river and drown myself. So then he took me up to the blacksmith's and had him make a hobble to fit my ankle and had a new trace chain run through it and riveted it around my leg. Then he had a long staple made to drive into the wall to lock me up to every night. Then they led me all over town just similar to a chained bear; they led me around to show me. Then Jimmy Benton came in that afternoon to take me up home with him. They took Phil out of jail but did not put any chains on him like they did me. He ran off that afternoon and hid himself in the barn and they did not get to take him home. His master was a better man than my master. So Benton took me home that evening and drove the staple in the wall and chained me up. My master told him to whip me every day if it was necessary, to whip me until he was satisfied, it did not make any difference if he killed me. He thought eighty dollars was a large amount of money to pay for one prisoner. That evening he got in his cowhides, straps and all of his whipping materials.

The next morning while I was sitting down to eat breakfast I heard a knock at the door. I opened it and there stood a troop of Union Home Guards. Some of them were some of the boys that I used to play with. So they took Jimmy Benton and put him in the same jail that I was formerly in. This same day they took John Bell Bruner and put him in prison across the river to Colonel Lilly's camp. I think they had been sympathizing with the rebels was the cause of this.

Jimmy Benton also had been taking sides with them. His father had a slave by the name of Jim Benton; he was a large fellow that weighed about one hundred and ninety pounds. This white Jimmy Benton had whipped this colored Jim until he could hardly lie in bed. This fellow had told on him is the reason they whipped him. Captain Shaunce told Jimmy Benton's wife to take me to the blacksmith shop and have those chains taken off of me as soon as she possibly could. This must have been the Providence of the Lord. So the blacksmith obeyed immediately and took the claims off of me at once.

I went on back to town as quick as I possibly could. I think after I had gone back to town I went back upon Miller's Creek, and there I worked at anything that I could find to do, if they would promise to pay me at night, so if it was necessary for me to go I would not leave anything behind. I got three dollars a day for cradling oats during harvest. The first time that I ever had a cradle in my hands in my life.

Old Henry Thomas lived right across the river from Benton's. He owned a large number of slaves. The old man died. He had three sons and two or three daughters. One of his sons was a minister and he married a poor girl and then his father deserted him and when he died only left him the pitiful sum of one dollar. About two weeks after the old man died his youngest son Mark undertook to whip one of their slaves by the name of Bolan Thomas. He accused the colored fellow of stealing because he found an empty sack in his cabin. It had just been two weeks exactly on this day (Saturday) since his father died, and he went in the house and loaded his gun and came out and killed this colored fellow, and this broke the will, but nothing was said about it no more than if he had been a dumb animal. Two weeks from the time that he murdered this slave, he was at the town of Irvine in a saloon, when Jack Steel and another gentleman became engaged in a quarrel, and this other man, I do not know his name, shot at Steel and as it happened missed him and shot Mark and killed him instantly, and so it was just a month's difference between the father's and son's death, and two weeks' difference between slave, father and son, and they all met their fate on Saturday. This Mark Thomas left a family to mourn his loss. He and Bolan were raised together on the same farm and were playmates all their short lives, when Mark had to commit this cruel deed for which he will never obtain forgiveness.

By this time I had gone back to Bruner's to live and work at the tanyard. Jimmy Benton and John Bell Bruner still remained in prison. After old Bruner did get out of prison he was very good indeed, he made me the most offers. He promised to give me half I made on the farm and give me half I made on the team on all the wood I would be fortunate enough to sell. And he also offered me the horse and buggy to take my girl to Wisemantown to meeting one Sunday, but I refused the offer. I thought that I would rather walk. They were getting most too good anyway, all of a sudden. So you know I knew there was something behind it for my mistress assisted me in putting my necktie on. That was the last Sunday that I spent near Irvin.

I then came back to Jonas Parks and remained all night, it was about a mile from home. The next morning about five o'clock I got up and started for Camp Nelson, which was forty-one miles from Irvin. And at eleven o'clock I had gone twenty-one miles and had arrived at Richmond. After I had left Richmond I came upon sixteen colored fellows who were on their way to Camp Nelson and of course I did not get lonesome. I had plenty of company. Just a half hour before sun down we arrived at Camp Nelson and had come forty-one miles in that day. The officers asked me what I wanted there and I told them that I came there to fight the rebels and that I wanted a gun. When I had run off before and wanted to go in the army and fight they said that they did not want any darkies, that this was a white man's war. After I had been there about a week they made up a regiment and called it the Twelfth U. S. Heavy Artillery.

I was enrolled on the twenty-fifth day of July in 1864 to serve three years or during the war, but I only remained two years and a half.

We started from Camp Nelson and marched eighteen miles that day and the dust was about four inches and my readers well know what nice walking it is when the dust is so very deep. When we got into the camp two or three dozen men fell out with the blind staggers, and I was in the midst of these unfortunate men.

The next morning we took the train for Louisville. When we arrived at Louisville that night we then took the freight train for Bowling Green and arrived there the next morning at about ten o'clock. A portion of the regiment took charge of Ft. Smith and a portion of Ft. Baker and some took charge of Ft. Vinegar. After we had been in the Camp two hours we than received orders to go to Russelville. We went there and went into stockyards, remained there a couple of days and the rebels were too hot for us, so we returned back and took charge of the Forts at Bowling Green, Ky. When we got back they made out a detail of fifty men to report to headquarters for duty and I was one of that number. When we got there we were given six days' provisions and eighty rounds of cartridges. In the meantime we had our knapsacks, tents and guns to carry with us.

Then we started on our journey from Bowling Green to Nashville, Tennessee, to guard a thousand head of cattle. Everything went well with us until we arrived at Franklin, Tennessee, except it rained on us every day. After we had passed into Franklin the next night we went into camp, everything began to go wrong. The food gave out and the rebels fired in on us. The rebels had three men to our one but they did not get any of our men or cattle. All of this occurred after night. We managed the next day to go to the mill to get some flour and when we cam back we made it up with water and put it on a board and held it up before the fire to bake it. We did not have any salt nor any shortening nor anything. That evening we found a hog that had five little pigs just about three days old and cleaned them and made soup of them. About that time that the soup was done the rebels fired in on us and made us go and forget all about our pig soup. So after this we did not have any more trouble until we reached Nashville with all of our cattle safe.

Our first Lieutenant of Company C was a man by the name of Wallace. He was a very brave man. After we went back to Bowling Green they took the same detail of men down to a station or a depot. There we laid on our guns all night and were not even allowed to whisper for the rebels were coming to burn the depot, but they did not come. After that I was detailed out to held on Fort Vinegar I had to help finish the fort and help make magazines. Then we had to go out four or five miles from town to cut timber to go over the magazines. Once or twice while I was out I took the chills and fever and was not able to go back to town, and I would be obliged to crawl into some man's barn and lay there all night, would not be able to get back to the camp. So one day the boys all stacked arms on the old Captain, his name was Toleman.

On account of not giving them their provisions he would take the food every Saturday and sell it and put the money in his pocket. So one day he sent a detail of one over to Fort Vinegar after me. He said I was the cause of the boys stacking arms, and took me before the Major, and when I arrived there the Major asked me what I knew about it and I informed him that I did not know anything about it for I had not been in camp for two weeks. Then the Major said that he would give me half an hour to make up my mind to tell the straight thing about it, and if I did not he would have me court martialed. I told him I did not have any education, that I did not know anything about stacking arms. So he sent me to the guard house, then he sent for me and I told him I did not know any more than I did the first time and that they could do what they wanted with me. So he sent me back to the Fort to where I was working and resumed my work. After that I took sick and had to be taken to the hospital and they looked for me to die every minute. After I got well they made me nurse in the hospital. So many men died, two and and three every night; I could not stand that so I went back to camp.

We camped out in little dog tents all winter. The tents were just large enough for two men to stay in, they were about four feet high. Often when we awakened in the morning we would be covered with snow. It blew into the tents and our blankets would be frozen to the ground so we could hardly get up. We carried our wood about a quarter of a mile.

One day while about eighteen miles from home recruiting we came to two or three large plantations. There were a great many colored people and as soon as they saw us they ran. We started after them and succeeded in capturing about 15 of the men. We started with our men and camped out at the foot of a hill and commenced to get supper when we were fired on by the rebels. This scared the recruits so bad we had gotten that they ran again. After this skirmish with the rebels, we coming out victorious, we caught our recruits and took them to camp. They cried, some of them, like babies and we had to let them go. "They had no time for war."

Their masters when they found out where they were, came after them. Instead of giving up we would keep them as prisoners and make them carry water. We have often had as high as twenty masters' prisoners, who came after their slaves (who came to us for protection). At one time we sent away five hundred men, women and children to Camp Nelson. Captain Palmer took us out one night. We marched about sixteen miles and about four o'clock the next morning we captured about 40 rebels without firing a gun. They all rode gray horses and wore old gray suits and without a doubt were the dirtiest men I ever saw on duty. Our Captain resigned his office and Lieutenant Wallace took charge of the Company. Our company took the train for Owensboro, Kentucky. When we arrived there the rebel citizens said that we should not remain there. Then a man by the name of John M. Hurd came and took charge of our Company at Owensboro, Kentucky. Once in a while we would go out and get a chicken and divide with our Captain but he did not care where we got them. Lieutenant Wallace would not allow the boys to take anything. He put one of the boys in the guard house for stealing a watermelon. So one day we thought we would go out and get some apples. We took a sack and got it full of apples. When I got back they took my apples and a revolver that cost twenty-five dollars and put me into the guard house, and I remained there, and then I got out and we went from Owensboro to Columbus, Kentucky. There were eight hundred men on the boat and we expected it to sink every minute. While we were at Columbus we did not do anything but drill and have a good time eating various kinds of fish. Then we moved from Columbus to Paducah, Kentucky. After we went up there they all took sick with the Measles in the Barracks, they had caught cold. While I was standing on guard facing the Ohio river on that cold New Year in 1865 my feet froze and they had to carry me off duty. My feet froze so badly that my toe nails came off. So when my feet got well we then took sick with the Smallpox and there were eleven men taken out of our company with this disease. One day I went out and bought some corn-bread from an old woman and she had the Smallpox. I did not know it and I took the Varioloid.

After I got well one night some fellows and I started up stairs to a dance and a colored fellow shot at me three times and missed me every time, but who the fellow was I did not know. I had never seen him before. So I thought it was about time I was shooting a little and I took my revolver out and shot at him and missed him and he ran. Then we went to Hopkinsville in Elton County and there we run some very narrow risks. We went down here to gather up the Government horses wherever we could find them. Sometimes the people that had them would not want to give them up, and when we had obtained these horses we would have to furnish something for them to eat.

One day I was sent out with a detail of three men to gather up the horses and everywhere that we found a horse with U. S. on it we would take it. So one Sunday we went out to forage some food for the horses. We went to two brothers houses, by the name of Chesnut, to get some hay and corn. One was a Union man and the other was a rebel. The Union man sent me to his brother and said that he had a large quantity, and he said that he did not have any and that his Union brother had some. So he gave us some cold ham and light bread and about a quart of whiskey and when we had disposed of these I told the boys to remain there. Then I went down about two hundred yards from the house and there I found three pens of corn and a large crib full and I rode over the field and there I found a large stack of oats. Then I made a colored fellow hitch up a wagon and yoke of oxen and haul a load of corn. Then I jumped upon the stack of oats and was throwing down oats when old Chesnut came out quarreling and said that he was going to report us to Sherman. I told him that he did not have anything to do with it. He said he did not have any so I just helped myself.

After that we were informed that at that same time there was a colored woman in bed that he had nearly beat to death. If we had known it we would have taken him too but we did not know it. So then we went back to Louisville, Kentucky, and was mustered out. Then I came up to Lexington and five of us hired a rockaway and came to Winchester and arrived there at one o'clock. I was at my mother's home then and we ate supper and my mother did not recognize me until after supper and then I made myself known. She would not believe it was her son. We had a very nice time after I made myself known. She heard that I was dead.

Then I hired a buggy and sent James Daniel up to Irvin to get my sister; she was still working for the white people and old Bruner would not let her come. She went out and made a fire and burnt up all of her bed clothing and put her foot in the road and walked and I never saw her until she came to Ohio. My old master sent word that he wanted to see me but I did not want to see him and I have never seen him since.

After the war I came to Ohio and have remained here ever since. My youngest sister, then living in Winchester, now dead; the other one came to Ohio several years back and died. My mother had not seen me for eighteen years. After I was mustered out of the army in 1866 I came to Oxford, Ohio, and went to live with my aunt and uncle, a family by the name of Brassfields. That winter I donated my money to them that I had made and went to school to Mr. Grennan. While I went to school I commenced getting a declamation and I was all winter getting it. I studied reading, writing, geography and spelling, and have not got it yet.

In the month of March I went out to work at David McDill's. I remained there until Fall and then my time had expired, so I came in and paid my board and started to school another winter. And then I began to study my piece again, and I never got my piece this winter. But once or twice a week I could spell some one down and get up head of the class. So I found out that that would not do and I was not learning anything so I thought I would quit going to school and get married.

I went to see a girl by the name of Fannie Procton, and finally we became engaged to be married. I went out in the country and cut wood and furnished a house and then we got married in March, 1868, and went out to live in the house which I had furnished. I went to work for a man by the name of Thomas Buck. It was way back in the woods, The farm is situated about 1 1/2 miles east of College Corner. After I had furnished my house and got my wife I just had 15 cents left to start on. I went in debt $42. The man I was working for gave me $26 a month. Old man Jeff Brown loaned me a cow and gave me a pig and Mr. Buck gave me a pig, and some of the neighbors gave me a hen and some a rooster and some a quantity of dried apples and various other things I will not mention, and then we were ready to make our fortune. We raised a great many chickens but the minks and rats caught a great many of them and then we did not have so many.

Every evening just before sun down my wife would become frightened and come up to Mr. Buck's. She said the house was haunted, but it was nothing but rats. Everything went on smoothly until harvest and I had been cutting wheat. I started away and I noticed a storm was coming up and so I returned to the house. I had no more than got to the house than twenty-five or thirty trees blew down in the woods. We were just through eating dinner and I undertook to shut the door and the wind blew the door down, and the window frames out, blew the roof off of the house and some logs off of the west side of the house, and blew the table over and broke some of the dishes. My wife and I were so scared we hardly knew where to go so we ran and jumped in the bed.

After the storm had ceased I went up and told Mr. Buck that he would have to move me out of there that I could not live in that old house and he said he would repair it which he did and we remained there until my time was out. When my time had expired I moved away. I had fifteen dollars ahead. When we moved from there we went and rented a couple of rooms from old Mr. East. Then I hired out to Tommy Roberts by the month. I hired to him for five months but only worked four, and during those four months the most I did was to cut wood, make rails and reset fences. I got $22 a month. The man lived seven miles from Oxford in Indiana. After I quit working out there I came in town and purchased a lot from widow Munns and gave $111.00 for it, and paid one-third down, and when I would go to pay the principal she would give me the interest back to buy dresses for my children. Tommy Roberts gave me an old house that Cale Nutt had given him. But the house would cost more than it was worth to move it, so I did not move that house.

At this time Mr. Roberts fooled me a little; he promised to loan me $25 and when I went to borrow it he went back on me. He had just invested all of his money in cattle, and then he said if I would find a man that would loan me the money he would go my security, but he would not even do that. So I was in debt about three hundred dollars. Then I hired to Jim Smith to work on the farm, and Palmer Smith, the man to whom the farm belonged, sold the farm to Mr. Ferris and that threw me out of employment.

About this time the Western Female Seminary burnt down, a college for girls a little distance from Oxford. So they hired me to help clean out the debris and help rebuild and do a great many other things. They gave me $1.50 per day and by this way I began to get out of debt. When the building was finished they hired me as night watchman for about three or four months and gave me $1.50 a night and I would work half of the day also. Mr. Lyons was Superintendent at this time. After school was out they hired me by the month and gave me $26 per month to do the chores, milk the cows and do various other things.

The next year I took charge of the boilers and heating apparatus. This was the year that General Grant ran for President against Horace Greely. So the girls thought they must have a jollification over the election. There was a number of the girls and two of them had to make a speech, one on the Democrat side and one on the Republican side and I had to draw them in a cart, the two speakers. And last I had to make a speech, one that will never be forgotton. The girls were so well pleased with my speech that they made up twenty-one dollars and bought me a velvet suit of clothes. My speech was put in the Harpers Weekly and some other papers at that time. Perhaps some of my dear readers have seen it.

I sold my house in town to John Givens. I had it pretty

Amidst Sunshine and Flowers, with Pipe and Happy Thoughts.

With His Two "Shadows," One of His Own Race,
the Other the Small Son of a Faculty Member.

PETER BRUNER
While, serving as janitor at Miami University.

A gala day for Peter Bruner! When President Taft
visited Miami University.

The Home of Hewn Logs Where Early Manhood
Years Were Lived.

A Larger Home Where the Family Grew and Prospered.

A Duet of Smiles, Grandfather and Grandson.

hard now as I was doing farming and small wages were paid. I decided to sell my house and buy in the country. I bought a house from Mr. East (a colored man) about a mile from town which I still own, and is very dear to me.

We lived in district No. 5. The teacher, a man by the name of Nort Greer, told me to send my two children who were then old enough to go to school, So I did as he directed me but the directors told the teacher not to teach them and so they were sent back home, because they were colored. But they later were compelled to teach them.

I went about $500 more in debt. I went up to Canada Brooks' and farmed for him about two years. Here I got a third of all I raised. The crops were poor and I had a very poor living.

Then I quit farming at Brooks' and went to work by the month for a man by the name of George Kramer, for $16 a month. I worked for him for two years; I was not getting out of debt very fast so I quit working at that place and went back to the Western Female Seminary in 1881 and hired under Wilber Peabody, who was then Superintendent. He gave me twenty-five dollars a month, house and my board; at this time I had two hundred dollars to raise and did not know how I was going to raise it. At last I heard of a man by the name of Charley Cook in Hamilton, Ohio, about twelve miles from Oxford, who had money to loan. I went to see this man and he said he would loan me the money providing that I would buy a lot from him and let him take a mortgage on both of the places. But I did not care to do that way. I thought that would not be getting out of debt, only getting farther in, so I refrained from borrowing money from this man. At last I came across Mr. John Fye and he said he would loan me two hundred dollars and take a mortgage on my property for two years at 6% interest, which he did. But I was able to refund the money before the two years had expired by working at the Western Seminary. I worked at this place as engineer for three years. I resigned this position in 1883 and moved out on my property which is located about one mile from Oxford, Ohio, on the College Corner pike.

After this I purchased a stone quarry from my mother-in-law and I sold a lot of stone from it. I sold it finally and got a job as engineer at the

Oxford College. Dr. Walker was president. It was while here I celebrated my 25th wedding anniversary in 1893. The teachers, faculty and seniors all agreed to make this a day never to be forgotten. They were invited to my home in the afternoon and they gave me many beautiful pieces of silver. At night we had a reception and invited our friends and we received many more beautiful presents.

I got a janitor job next under Dr. Thompson at Miami University, and while here made many substantial friends. I worked here 13 years under Presidents Tappen and Benton. I had the pleasure of waiting on President Taft while employed at Miami[.]

In 1886 our home was made sad when our little baby thirteen months old was taken.

Two of my daughters having married, and with my work in town I decided to bring the rest of my family, two more girls and my wife, to town. So I bought the house where I now live. I have been a member of Bethel A. M. E. church for over fifty years, having joined the church under Rev. Stonewall Jackson.

In 1918 my wife and I had the pleasure of celebrating our Golden Anniversary. We again had a reception and had many of our friends to help us celebrate the occasion. Again we were kindly remembered.

In 1900 God saw fit to take my second daughter, Carrie, the one who wrote this book when she was a girl. Many many nights she spent over it. The book was lost awhile and it was not until my house was burned in August, 1913, that the book was again discovered. We feel God has wonderfully blessed us.

Though my life has been one of many hardships, I feel there awaits for me a crown of righteousness, and I shall have rest forever more.

PETER BRUNER

By EDNA BRADLEY
(Granddaughter)

Up from Kentucky in days that were dark,
Came Peter Bruner on the wings of a stork.
Tho' born as a slave in a little log shack,
 He was keen as a squirrel and sharp as a tack.

No sports did he play, like the boys of today,
But worked and toiled with a lash for his pay,

By the hand of a master,
Who was drunk night and day.

But he waxed and grew strong like a tree,
Till Abraham Lincoln, the president to be.
Sent out the word, that all men could fight
And Peter hurried forth away in the night.

Then in the year "65" all men were set free,
As God in heaven intended it should be.

For the Bible tells us and so does "Paul"
That God's the Father of us all.

After Peter was set free, to Oxford he came,
To find a wife or probably fame.
But 'twas in Fanny Proctor's heart
Dan Cupid thrust his loving dart.

In the year "68" this couple was tied
In wedlock, so happy and gay.
And lo! in a year a baby appeared,
'Twas Alice, the babe full of play.

Then Carrie the babe with a winsome smile,
Came to brighten this home awhile.
And Stella arrived in a few years more,
Her voice full of gay, childish lore.

Then the home was saddened by Goldie Fay,
When God's angel took her away.
But then came the last of the baby girls,
Frances Mildred with a head full of curls.

This happy pair have lived to share
Many joys and sorrows and care.
But God has been good, and protected this home
With fifty-seven wedded years to roam.

Thus after all is said and done,
After many joys and lots of fun,
The greatest thing in this "here" poem,
Is Peter Bruner's happy home.

www.ingramcontent.com/pod-product-compliance
Lightning Source LLC
Chambersburg PA
CBHW080053280326
41934CB00014B/3299